Muhammad Ali

Julia Holt

Published in association with The Basic Skills Agency

Hodder & Stoughton

A MEMBER OF THE HODDER HEADLINE GROUP

Acknowledgements

Photos: p. iv © Retna Pictures, pp. 3, 19 © Corbis, pp. 6, 9, 25 © Allsport,
      pp. 16, 22 © Camera Press Ltd.
Cover photo: © Popperfoto.

Orders: please contact Bookpoint Ltd, 39 Milton Park, Abingdon, Oxon OX14 4TD. Telephone: (44)
01235 400414, Fax: (44) 01235 400454. Lines are open from 9.00–6.00, Monday to Saturday, with a
24 hour message answering service. Email address: orders@bookpoint.co.uk

British Library Cataloguing in Publication Data
A catalogue record for this title is available from The British Library

ISBN 0 340 72065 4

First published 1994
Impression number 10 9 8 7 6 5 4
Year 2003 2002 2001 2000

Copyright © 1994 The Basic Skills Agency.

Typeset by Fakenham Photosetting Ltd, Fakenham, Norfolk.
Printed in Great Britain for Hodder & Stoughton Educational, a division of Hodder Headline Plc,
338 Euston Road, London NW1 3BH by Redwood Books, Trowbridge, Wiltshire.

Contents

There is a man
who has had two different names.
He is world famous
with both of them.

He floats like a butterfly,
stings like a bee,
he is the greatest,
Muhammad Ali.

1 Early Days

One day in 1954,
at the age of 12,
Cassius Clay went into town
on his bike.

His bike was stolen
and he went into a nearby gym
to get help.

He saw men boxing
and he became interested.

Clay started to train.
His trainer was the local policeman,
Joe Martin.

He worked very hard.
Six weeks later
he won his first fight.
He weighed 89 pounds.
After the fight
he started shouting:
'I am going to be
the greatest fighter ever.'

Clay worked his way up
through the amateur ranks.
He became so good
that he boxed
in the 1960 Rome Olympics.
Clay won the gold medal.

Clay knew
he could make a living
as a professional boxer.

He could make the money
he needed for his family.

So, in 1960,
he became a professional boxer
and a showman.
He had very fast feet
and a big mouth.

He became known
for his personality.
He said 'I am the greatest',
and he meant it.

In 1963
Clay came to England
to fight Henry Cooper.

He came into the ring
in a red coat
and a golden crown.

He said he would win
in round five,
and he did.
But not before
Cooper knocked him down
in round four
just before the bell.

VIEWSPORT LTD IN ASSOCIATION WITH RANK PROUDLY

THE FIGHT OF THE
ON LARGE
THEAT
FROM THE
THE HEAVYWEIG

2 Heavy-weight Champion

Clay wanted to win
the heavy-weight world title.

So in February 1964
he fought Sonny Liston.

Liston was a boxer
to be feared.
He had been in prison
for armed robbery.
People said that
Clay did not have a chance.
This did not stop him
from calling Liston
a big ugly bear.

Clay used his speed
to out-box Liston.
At the end of round six
Liston stopped boxing.
He sat on his stool
and said his shoulder hurt.

Clay became
the heavy-weight champion
of the world.
It was one of the biggest upsets
in boxing history.

But some people said
the fight was a fix.

After the fight
Clay told the newspapers
that he was a Muslim.

In March 1964,
he took the name
Muhammad Ali.
He dropped his old name
because it was a slave's name.

Ali joined
the Nation of Islam.
They said black people
should resist white power.

After this,
Ali was not so popular
with some people.

In 1964
Ali got married.
Sonji was the first
of his four wives.
They were divorced
after two years.

For the next three years
Ali was at the top of his form.
He became the fastest champion
of all time.

Ali fought Liston again
in 1965.
The fight lasted 60 seconds.
He knocked Liston out
with a blow to his chin.

The blow was so fast
that no-one saw it.
So they said it was a fix again.

Ali defended his title
ten times, between 1964 and 1967.
This is more
than any other heavy-weight champion
has ever done.

He said 'I can't be hit.
There's not a man on earth
with the speed
and ability to beat me.'

3 The Vietnam War

Ali was on top of the world
but in April 1967
he was told to join the army.

America was fighting a war
in Vietnam.
Ali said
he had nothing against the Vietcong.
He said he was a Muslim
and he would not go to war.

He was fined $10,000
and his world title
was taken away.

For the next three years
he was not allowed to fight.

The ban was a big blow to Ali.
He lost three of his best boxing years
because of his beliefs.

His choice
had a big impact
on people everywhere.

It made them think again
about the Vietnam war.

In the meantime
Joe Frazier became the champion.

Ali carried on with his life.
He married
17 year old Belinda in 1967
and they had four children.

4 Come-back

In October 1970
the courts let Ali fight again.
He won his first two fights
but he was slower than before.

Because he was slower
he got hit badly,
for the first time.

In March 1971
Joe Frazier knocked Ali down
in round 15.
For the first time,
Ali lost a fight.

He won his next 10 fights.

Then in March 1973
he fought Ken Norton.
Norton broke Ali's jaw
in round two.
Ali stayed on his feet
for 10 more rounds.
In the end
Norton won the fight.

Now all Ali wanted to do
was to fight Frazier and Norton again.

He did
and he won both fights.

5 Heavy-weight Champion Again

Ali wanted his title back.
He had to fight George Forman,
in Africa in 1974.

This was the famous
'Rumble in the Jungle'.
Before the fight, Ali said:
'I float like a butterfly,
sting like a bee,
his hands can't hit
what his eyes can't see'.

Again Ali was the under-dog
but he had a plan.
He let Forman
tire himself out.

Ali won by a knockout
in round eight.
Seven years after
his title was taken away
he won it back.

He was 32 years old.
He had done the impossible
and got his title back.

Over the next three years
Ali had 10 fights.
He won them all.

One of those fights
in 1975
was the fight of his life.
It was called 'The Thriller in Manilla'.
It was his third fight
against Joe Frazier.

Everybody said
that Frazier was finished
and the fight would be easy for Ali.
But it wasn't.

Ali won,
but not before
Frazier landed 440 blows,
mostly to Ali's head.

It was a good time
for Ali to retire,
but he didn't.

Ali lost his title
in February 1978
to Leon Spinks.

Seven months later
he pulled himself together
and won it back.

Ali is the only man ever
to win the heavy-weight title
three times.

6 The Record

Ali stopped boxing in 1981.
His career lasted 21 years.
He had 56 wins
with 37 knockouts.

He lost only five times.

Muhammad Ali did a lot
to make boxing popular.
The sport will never be the same
without him.

He is the greatest.

7 Ali Today

Children are a big part
of Ali's life.
He had two girls
with his third wife Veronica.

In total he had
seven girls
and one boy.

Then in 1986
he married his fourth wife Lonnie.
Today they live on a farm
in Michigan.

They adopted a baby boy
called Asaad in 1991.
He is the apple
of his father's eye.

Sadly, Ali now has brain damage
from all the blows he took
to his head.

This means
his speech is slurred
and his hands tremble.
But it has not
affected his mind.
His mind is still
razor sharp.

In 1996,
in front of 3.5 billion people,
he lit the Olympic flame in Atlanta.

Everyone watching was moved.
After, he sat in his hotel
just looking at the torch.
He was moved
by everyone willing him on.

In 1997 a film came out
called 'When We Were Kings'.

It was about
the 'Rumble in the Jungle'.
In the film we get to see again
Ali the great fighter.

He is still loved and respected
all round the world.
He will always be the greatest.

He still travels the world.
He still signs
2,000 autographs a week.

And he still wants to know
who stole his bike
back in 1954.